My Yearly Saving Goal

I will save_____ this year.

I want to save this for_____

I will do this by_____

I0472023

Use the saving tracker to help you keep track of your goal. There are 400 squares

Every square equals_____ saved.

My Saving Tracker

My Ongoing Bill Schedule

Bill	Cost	Due

Month Of: 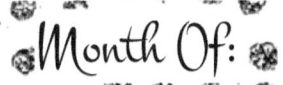 _____ / 20

Income

	Expected	Actual
Income #1 (after tax)		
Income #2 (after tax)		
Other (after tax)		

Expenses

	Budgeted	Actual
Travel (fuel/bus/train)		
Totals		
	Leftover	

My Monthly Saving

Goal	Actual	Notes

One Off Expenses This Month

Expense	Cost	Due

Planned Treats

Treat	Budgeted	Actual Cost	Date

Totals

Money in	Money Out	Money Leftover

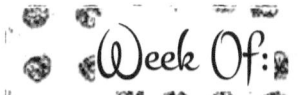

Track everything you spend each day. This will help you see things you might be able to cut down on so you can reach your saving goals.

Monday Expense	Cost
Total:	

Tuesday Expense	Cost
Total:	

Wednesday Expense	Cost
Total:	

Thursday Expense	Cost
Total:	

Friday

Expense	Cost
Total:	

Saturday

Expense	Cost
Total:	

Sunday

Expense	Cost
Total:	

Notes

Things To Cut Down

Expense	Potential Saving

Week Of: _____ / 20

Track everything you spend each day. This will help you see things you might be able to cut down on so you can reach your saving goals.

Monday

Expense	Cost
Total:	

Tuesday

Expense	Cost
Total:	

Wednesday

Expense	Cost
Total:	

Thursday

Expense	Cost
Total:	

Friday

Expense	Cost
Total:	

Saturday

Expense	Cost
Total:	

Sunday

Expense	Cost
Total:	

Notes

Things To Cut Down

Expense	Potential Saving

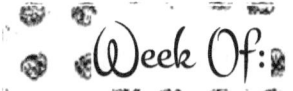 Week Of: _____ / 20

Track everything you spend each day. This will help you see things you might be able to cut down on so you can reach your saving goals.

Monday

Expense	Cost
Total:	

Tuesday

Expense	Cost
Total:	

Wednesday

Expense	Cost
Total:	

Thursday

Expense	Cost
Total:	

Friday

Expense	Cost
Total:	

Saturday

Expense	Cost
Total:	

Sunday

Expense	Cost
Total:	

Notes

Things To Cut Down

Expense	Potential Saving

 Week Of: _____ / 20

Track everything you spend each day. This will help you see things you might be able to cut down on so you can reach your saving goals.

Monday

Expense	Cost
Total:	

Tuesday

Expense	Cost
Total:	

Wednesday

Expense	Cost
Total:	

Thursday

Expense	Cost
Total:	

Friday

Expense	Cost
Total:	

Saturday

Expense	Cost
Total:	

Sunday

Expense	Cost
Total:	

Notes

Things To Cut Down

Expense	Potential Saving

Month Of: _____ / 20

Income

	Expected	Actual
Income #1 (after tax)		
Income #2 (after tax)		
Other (after tax)		

Expenses

	Budgeted	Actual
Travel (fuel/bus/train)		
Totals		
	Leftover	

My Monthly Saving

Goal	Actual	Notes

One Off Expenses This Month

Expense	Cost	Due

Planned Treats

Treat	Budgeted	Actual Cost	Date

Totals

Money in	Money Out	Money Leftover

Track everything you spend each day. This will help you see things you might be able to cut down on so you can reach your saving goals.

Monday

Expense	Cost
Total:	

Tuesday

Expense	Cost
Total:	

Wednesday

Expense	Cost
Total:	

Thursday

Expense	Cost
Total:	

Friday

Expense	Cost
Total:	

Saturday

Expense	Cost
Total:	

Sunday

Expense	Cost
Total:	

Notes

Things To Cut Down

Expense	Potential Saving

 Week Of: _____

/ 20

Track everything you spend each day. This will help you see things you might be able to cut down on so you can reach your saving goals.

Monday

Expense	Cost
Total:	

Tuesday

Expense	Cost
Total:	

Wednesday

Expense	Cost
Total:	

Thursday

Expense	Cost
Total:	

Friday

Expense	Cost
Total:	

Saturday

Expense	Cost
Total:	

Sunday

Expense	Cost
Total:	

Notes

| |
| |
| |
| |
| |
| |
| |

Things To Cut Down

Expense	Potential Saving

Week Of: _____ / 20

Track everything you spend each day. This will help you see things you might be able to cut down on so you can reach your saving goals.

Monday

Expense	Cost
Total:	

Tuesday

Expense	Cost
Total:	

Wednesday

Expense	Cost
Total:	

Thursday

Expense	Cost
Total:	

Friday

Expense	Cost
	Total:

Saturday

Expense	Cost
	Total:

Sunday

Expense	Cost
	Total:

Notes

Things To Cut Down

Expense	Potential Saving

 Week Of: _____

Track everything you spend each day. This will help you see things you might be able to cut down on so you can reach your saving goals.

Monday

Expense	Cost
Total:	

Tuesday

Expense	Cost
Total:	

Wednesday

Expense	Cost
Total:	

Thursday

Expense	Cost
Total:	

Friday

Expense	Cost
Total:	

Saturday

Expense	Cost
Total:	

Sunday

Expense	Cost
Total:	

Notes

Things To Cut Down

Expense	Potential Saving

 Month Of: _____   / 20

Income

	Expected	Actual
Income #1 (after tax)		
Income #2 (after tax)		
Other (after tax)		

Expenses

	Budgeted	Actual
Travel (fuel/bus/train)		
Totals		
	Leftover	

My Monthly Saving

Goal	Actual	Notes

One Off Expenses This Month

Expense	Cost	Due

Planned Treats

Treat	Budgeted	Actual Cost	Date

Totals

Money in	Money Out	Money Leftover

Track everything you spend each day. This will help you see things you might be able to cut down on so you can reach your saving goals.

Monday	
Expense	Cost
Total:	

Tuesday	
Expense	Cost
Total:	

Wednesday	
Expense	Cost
Total:	

Thursday	
Expense	Cost
Total:	

Friday

Expense	Cost
Total:	

Saturday

Expense	Cost
Total:	

Sunday

Expense	Cost
Total:	

Notes

Things To Cut Down

Expense	Potential Saving

Track everything you spend each day. This will help you see things you might be able to cut down on so you can reach your saving goals.

Monday

Expense	Cost
Total:	

Tuesday

Expense	Cost
Total:	

Wednesday

Expense	Cost
Total:	

Thursday

Expense	Cost
Total:	

Friday

Expense	Cost
Total:	

Saturday

Expense	Cost
Total:	

Sunday

Expense	Cost
Total:	

Notes

Things To Cut Down

Expense	Potential Saving

Week Of: _____ / 20

Track everything you spend each day. This will help you see things you might be able to cut down on so you can reach your saving goals.

Monday

Expense	Cost
Total:	

Tuesday

Expense	Cost
Total:	

Wednesday

Expense	Cost
Total:	

Thursday

Expense	Cost
Total:	

Friday

Expense	Cost
Total:	

Saturday

Expense	Cost
Total:	

Sunday

Expense	Cost
Total:	

Notes

Things To Cut Down

Expense	Potential Saving

Week Of: _____ / 20

Track everything you spend each day. This will help you see things you might be able to cut down on so you can reach your saving goals.

Monday

Expense	Cost
Total:	

Tuesday

Expense	Cost
Total:	

Wednesday

Expense	Cost
Total:	

Thursday

Expense	Cost
Total:	

Friday

Expense	Cost
Total:	

Saturday

Expense	Cost
Total:	

Sunday

Expense	Cost
Total:	

Notes

| |
| |
| |
| |
| |
| |
| |

Things To Cut Down

Expense	Potential Saving

Three Month Review

When I think about money, I feel...

_____

_____

_____

Saved So Far

Average Daily Spend

Average Monthly Spend

Things I've Cut Down On

Expense	Old Cost	Cost now

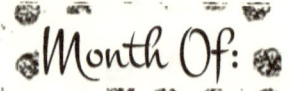 Month Of: _____ / 20

Income

	Expected	Actual
Income #1 (after tax)		
Income #2 (after tax)		
Other (after tax)		

Expenses

	Budgeted	Actual
Travel (fuel/bus/train)		
Totals		
	Leftover	

My Monthly Saving

Goal	Actual	Notes

One Off Expenses This Month

Expense	Cost	Due

Planned Treats

Treat	Budgeted	Actual Cost	Date

Totals

Money in	Money Out	Money Leftover

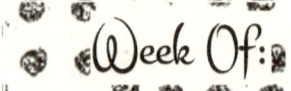

Track everything you spend each day. This will help you see things you might be able to cut down on so you can reach your saving goals.

Monday

Expense	Cost
Total:	

Tuesday

Expense	Cost
Total:	

Wednesday

Expense	Cost
Total:	

Thursday

Expense	Cost
Total:	

Friday

Expense	Cost
Total:	

Saturday

Expense	Cost
Total:	

Sunday

Expense	Cost
Total:	

Notes

Things To Cut Down

Expense	Potential Saving

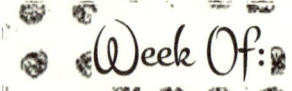

Track everything you spend each day. This will help you see things you might be able to cut down on so you can reach your saving goals.

Monday

Expense	Cost
Total:	

Tuesday

Expense	Cost
Total:	

Wednesday

Expense	Cost
Total:	

Thursday

Expense	Cost
Total:	

Friday

Expense	Cost
Total:	

Saturday

Expense	Cost
Total:	

Sunday

Expense	Cost
Total:	

Notes

Things To Cut Down

Expense	Potential Saving

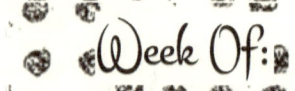

Track everything you spend each day. This will help you see things you might be able to cut down on so you can reach your saving goals.

Monday	
Expense	Cost
Total:	

Tuesday	
Expense	Cost
Total:	

Wednesday	
Expense	Cost
Total:	

Thursday	
Expense	Cost
Total:	

Friday

Expense	Cost
Total:	

Saturday

Expense	Cost
Total:	

Sunday

Expense	Cost
Total:	

Notes

Things To Cut Down

Expense	Potential Saving

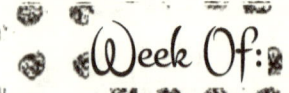

Week Of:

Track everything you spend each day. This will help you see things you might be able to cut down on so you can reach your saving goals.

Monday

Expense	Cost
Total:	

Tuesday

Expense	Cost
Total:	

Wednesday

Expense	Cost
Total:	

Thursday

Expense	Cost
Total:	

Friday

Expense	Cost
Total:	

Saturday

Expense	Cost
Total:	

Sunday

Expense	Cost
Total:	

Notes

Things To Cut Down

Expense	Potential Saving

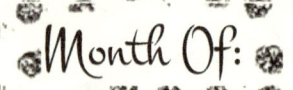 Month Of: _____ / 20

Income

	Expected	Actual
Income #1 (after tax)		
Income #2 (after tax)		
Other (after tax)		

Expenses

	Budgeted	Actual
Travel (fuel/bus/train)		
Totals		
	Leftover	

My Monthly Saving

Goal	Actual	Notes

One Off Expenses This Month

Expense	Cost	Due

Planned Treats

Treat	Budgeted	Actual Cost	Date

Totals

Money in	Money Out	Money Leftover

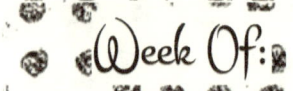

Track everything you spend each day. This will help you see things you might be able to cut down on so you can reach your saving goals.

Monday

Expense	Cost
Total:	

Tuesday

Expense	Cost
Total:	

Wednesday

Expense	Cost
Total:	

Thursday

Expense	Cost
Total:	

Friday

Expense	Cost
Total:	

Saturday

Expense	Cost
Total:	

Sunday

Expense	Cost
Total:	

Notes

Things To Cut Down

Expense	Potential Saving

Week Of: _____ / 20

Track everything you spend each day. This will help you see things you might be able to cut down on so you can reach your saving goals.

Monday

Expense	Cost
Total:	

Tuesday

Expense	Cost
Total:	

Wednesday

Expense	Cost
Total:	

Thursday

Expense	Cost
Total:	

Friday

Expense	Cost
Total:	

Saturday

Expense	Cost
Total:	

Sunday

Expense	Cost
Total:	

Notes

Things To Cut Down

Expense	Potential Saving

Week Of: / 20

Track everything you spend each day. This will help you see things you might be able to cut down on so you can reach your saving goals.

Monday

Expense	Cost
Total:	

Tuesday

Expense	Cost
Total:	

Wednesday

Expense	Cost
Total:	

Thursday

Expense	Cost
Total:	

Friday

Expense	Cost
Total:	

Saturday

Expense	Cost
Total:	

Sunday

Expense	Cost
Total:	

Notes

Things To Cut Down

Expense	Potential Saving

Week Of:

Track everything you spend each day. This will help you see things you might be able to cut down on so you can reach your saving goals.

Monday

Expense	Cost
Total:	

Tuesday

Expense	Cost
Total:	

Wednesday

Expense	Cost
Total:	

Thursday

Expense	Cost
Total:	

Friday

Expense	Cost
Total:	

Saturday

Expense	Cost
Total:	

Sunday

Expense	Cost
Total:	

Notes

Things To Cut Down

Expense	Potential Saving

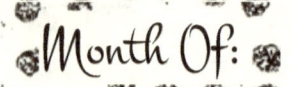

Month Of: _____

Income

	Expected	Actual
Income #1 (after tax)		
Income #2 (after tax)		
Other (after tax)		

Expenses

	Budgeted	Actual
Travel (fuel/bus/train)		
Totals		
	Leftover	

My Monthly Saving

Goal	Actual	Notes

One Off Expenses This Month

Expense	Cost	Due

Planned Treats

Treat	Budgeted	Actual Cost	Date

Totals

Money in	Money Out	Money Leftover

Week Of: / 20

Track everything you spend each day. This will help you see things you might be able to cut down on so you can reach your saving goals.

Monday

Expense	Cost
Total:	

Tuesday

Expense	Cost
Total:	

Wednesday

Expense	Cost
Total:	

Thursday

Expense	Cost
Total:	

Friday

Expense	Cost
Total:	

Saturday

Expense	Cost
Total:	

Sunday

Expense	Cost
Total:	

Notes

Things To Cut Down

Expense	Potential Saving

Week Of: _____ / 20

Track everything you spend each day. This will help you see things you might be able to cut down on so you can reach your saving goals.

Monday

Expense	Cost
Total:	

Tuesday

Expense	Cost
Total:	

Wednesday

Expense	Cost
Total:	

Thursday

Expense	Cost
Total:	

Friday

Expense	Cost
Total:	

Saturday

Expense	Cost
Total:	

Sunday

Expense	Cost
Total:	

Notes

Things To Cut Down

Expense	Potential Saving

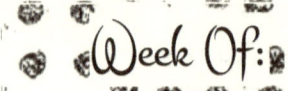 Week Of: _____ / 20

Track everything you spend each day. This will help you see things you might be able to cut down on so you can reach your saving goals.

Monday

Expense	Cost
Total:	

Tuesday

Expense	Cost
Total:	

Wednesday

Expense	Cost
Total:	

Thursday

Expense	Cost
Total:	

Friday

Expense	Cost
Total:	

Saturday

Expense	Cost
Total:	

Sunday

Expense	Cost
Total:	

Notes

Things To Cut Down

Expense	Potential Saving

Track everything you spend each day. This will help you see things you might be able to cut down on so you can reach your saving goals.

Monday

Expense	Cost
Total:	

Tuesday

Expense	Cost
Total:	

Wednesday

Expense	Cost
Total:	

Thursday

Expense	Cost
Total:	

Friday

Expense	Cost
Total:	

Saturday

Expense	Cost
Total:	

Sunday

Expense	Cost
Total:	

Notes

Things To Cut Down

Expense	Potential Saving

Six Month Review

When I think about money, I feel...

_____

_____

_____

Saved So Far

Average Daily Spend

Average Monthly Spend

Things I've Cut Down On

Expense	Old Cost	Cost now

Month Of: _____ / 20

Income

	Expected	Actual
Income #1 (after tax)		
Income #2 (after tax)		
Other (after tax)		

Expenses

	Budgeted	Actual
Travel (fuel/bus/train)		
Totals		
	Leftover	

My Monthly Saving

Goal	Actual	Notes

One Off Expenses This Month

Expense	Cost	Due

Planned Treats

Treat	Budgeted	Actual Cost	Date

Totals

Money in	Money Out	Money Leftover

 **Week Of:** _____ **/ 20**

Track everything you spend each day. This will help you see things you might be able to cut down on so you can reach your saving goals.

Monday	
Expense	Cost
Total:	

Tuesday	
Expense	Cost
Total:	

Wednesday	
Expense	Cost
Total:	

Thursday	
Expense	Cost
Total:	

Friday

Expense	Cost
Total:	

Saturday

Expense	Cost
Total:	

Sunday

Expense	Cost
Total:	

Notes

Things To Cut Down

Expense	Potential Saving

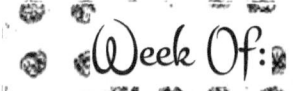

Track everything you spend each day. This will help you see things you might be able to cut down on so you can reach your saving goals.

Monday	
Expense	Cost
Total:	

Tuesday	
Expense	Cost
Total:	

Wednesday	
Expense	Cost
Total:	

Thursday	
Expense	Cost
Total:	

Friday

Expense	Cost
Total:	

Saturday

Expense	Cost
Total:	

Sunday

Expense	Cost
Total:	

Notes

Things To Cut Down

Expense	Potential Saving

Track everything you spend each day. This will help you see things you might be able to cut down on so you can reach your saving goals.

Monday

Expense	Cost
Total:	

Tuesday

Expense	Cost
Total:	

Wednesday

Expense	Cost
Total:	

Thursday

Expense	Cost
Total:	

Friday

Expense	Cost
Total:	

Saturday

Expense	Cost
Total:	

Sunday

Expense	Cost
Total:	

Notes

Things To Cut Down

Expense	Potential Saving

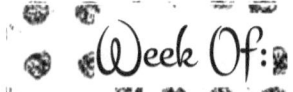

Track everything you spend each day. This will help you see things you might be able to cut down on so you can reach your saving goals.

Monday Expense	Cost
Total:	

Tuesday Expense	Cost
Total:	

Wednesday Expense	Cost
Total:	

Thursday Expense	Cost
Total:	

Friday

Expense	Cost
Total:	

Saturday

Expense	Cost
Total:	

Sunday

Expense	Cost
Total:	

Notes

Things To Cut Down

Expense	Potential Saving

Month Of: _____ / 20

Income

	Expected	Actual
Income #1 (after tax)		
Income #2 (after tax)		
Other (after tax)		

Expenses

	Budgeted	Actual
Travel (fuel/bus/train)		
Totals		
	Leftover	

My Monthly Saving

Goal	Actual	Notes

One Off Expenses This Month

Expense	Cost	Due

Planned Treats

Treat	Budgeted	Actual Cost	Date

Totals

Money in	Money Out	Money Leftover

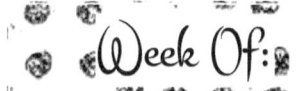 Week Of:

Track everything you spend each day. This will help you see things you might be able to cut down on so you can reach your saving goals.

Monday

Expense	Cost
Total:	

Tuesday

Expense	Cost
Total:	

Wednesday

Expense	Cost
Total:	

Thursday

Expense	Cost
Total:	

Friday

Expense	Cost
Total:	

Saturday

Expense	Cost
Total:	

Sunday

Expense	Cost
Total:	

Notes

Things To Cut Down

Expense	Potential Saving

 Week Of: _____ / 20

Track everything you spend each day. This will help you see things you might be able to cut down on so you can reach your saving goals.

Monday

Expense	Cost
Total:	

Tuesday

Expense	Cost
Total:	

Wednesday

Expense	Cost
Total:	

Thursday

Expense	Cost
Total:	

Friday

Expense	Cost
Total:	

Saturday

Expense	Cost
Total:	

Sunday

Expense	Cost
Total:	

Notes

Things To Cut Down

Expense	Potential Saving

Track everything you spend each day. This will help you see things you might be able to cut down on so you can reach your saving goals.

Monday	
Expense	Cost
Total:	

Tuesday	
Expense	Cost
Total:	

Wednesday	
Expense	Cost
Total:	

Thursday	
Expense	Cost
Total:	

Friday

Expense	Cost
Total:	

Saturday

Expense	Cost
Total:	

Sunday

Expense	Cost
Total:	

Notes

Things To Cut Down

Expense	Potential Saving

Track everything you spend each day. This will help you see things you might be able to cut down on so you can reach your saving goals.

Monday

Expense	Cost
Total:	

Tuesday

Expense	Cost
Total:	

Wednesday

Expense	Cost
Total:	

Thursday

Expense	Cost
Total:	

Friday

Expense	Cost
Total:	

Saturday

Expense	Cost
Total:	

Sunday

Expense	Cost
Total:	

Notes

Things To Cut Down

Expense	Potential Saving

Month Of: _____ / 20

Income

	Expected	Actual
Income #1 (after tax)		
Income #2 (after tax)		
Other (after tax)		

Expenses

	Budgeted	Actual
Travel (fuel/bus/train)		
Totals		
	Leftover	

My Monthly Saving

Goal	Actual	Notes

One Off Expenses This Month

Expense	Cost	Due

Planned Treats

Treat	Budgeted	Actual Cost	Date

Totals

Money in	Money Out	Money Leftover

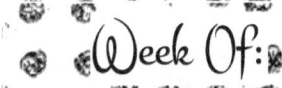

Track everything you spend each day. This will help you see things you might be able to cut down on so you can reach your saving goals.

Monday Expense	Cost
Total:	

Tuesday Expense	Cost
Total:	

Wednesday Expense	Cost
Total:	

Thursday Expense	Cost
Total:	

Friday

Expense	Cost
Total:	

Saturday

Expense	Cost
Total:	

Sunday

Expense	Cost
Total:	

Notes

Things To Cut Down

Expense	Potential Saving

 Week Of: / 20

Track everything you spend each day. This will help you see things you might be able to cut down on so you can reach your saving goals.

Monday

Expense	Cost
Total:	

Tuesday

Expense	Cost
Total:	

Wednesday

Expense	Cost
Total:	

Thursday

Expense	Cost
Total:	

Friday

Expense	Cost
Total:	

Saturday

Expense	Cost
Total:	

Sunday

Expense	Cost
Total:	

Notes

Things To Cut Down

Expense	Potential Saving

Track everything you spend each day. This will help you see things you might be able to cut down on so you can reach your saving goals.

Monday

Expense	Cost
Total:	

Tuesday

Expense	Cost
Total:	

Wednesday

Expense	Cost
Total:	

Thursday

Expense	Cost
Total:	

Friday

Expense	Cost
Total:	

Saturday

Expense	Cost
Total:	

Sunday

Expense	Cost
Total:	

Notes

Things To Cut Down

Expense	Potential Saving

Week Of: _____ / 20

Track everything you spend each day. This will help you see things you might be able to cut down on so you can reach your saving goals.

Monday

Expense	Cost
Total:	

Tuesday

Expense	Cost
Total:	

Wednesday

Expense	Cost
Total:	

Thursday

Expense	Cost
Total:	

Friday

Expense	Cost
Total:	

Saturday

Expense	Cost
Total:	

Sunday

Expense	Cost
Total:	

Notes

Things To Cut Down

Expense	Potential Saving

Nine Month Review

When I think about money, I feel...

_____

_____

_____

Saved So Far

Average Daily Spend

Average Monthly Spend

Things I've Cut Down On

Expense	Old Cost	Cost now

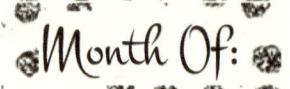

Month Of: _____ / 20

Income

	Expected	Actual
Income #1 (after tax)		
Income #2 (after tax)		
Other (after tax)		

Expenses

	Budgeted	Actual
Travel (fuel/bus/train)		
Totals		
	Leftover	

My Monthly Saving

Goal	Actual	Notes

One Off Expenses This Month

Expense	Cost	Due

Planned Treats

Treat	Budgeted	Actual Cost	Date

Totals

Money in	Money Out	Money Leftover

Track everything you spend each day. This will help you see things you might be able to cut down on so you can reach your saving goals.

Monday	
Expense	Cost
Total:	

Tuesday	
Expense	Cost
Total:	

Wednesday	
Expense	Cost
Total:	

Thursday	
Expense	Cost
Total:	

Friday

Expense	Cost
Total:	

Saturday

Expense	Cost
Total:	

Sunday

Expense	Cost
Total:	

Notes

Things To Cut Down

Expense	Potential Saving

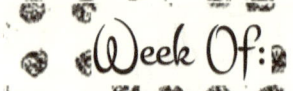

Week Of: / 20

Track everything you spend each day. This will help you see things you might be able to cut down on so you can reach your saving goals.

Monday

Expense	Cost
Total:	

Tuesday

Expense	Cost
Total:	

Wednesday

Expense	Cost
Total:	

Thursday

Expense	Cost
Total:	

Friday

Expense	Cost
Total:	

Saturday

Expense	Cost
Total:	

Sunday

Expense	Cost
Total:	

Notes

| |
| |
| |
| |
| |
| |

Things To Cut Down

Expense	Potential Saving

Week Of: _____ / 20

Track everything you spend each day. This will help you see things you might be able to cut down on so you can reach your saving goals.

Monday

Expense	Cost
Total:	

Tuesday

Expense	Cost
Total:	

Wednesday

Expense	Cost
Total:	

Thursday

Expense	Cost
Total:	

Friday

Expense	Cost
Total:	

Saturday

Expense	Cost
Total:	

Sunday

Expense	Cost
Total:	

Notes

| |
| |
| |
| |
| |
| |
| |

Things To Cut Down

Expense	Potential Saving

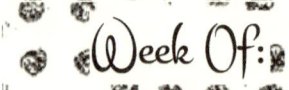

Track everything you spend each day. This will help you see things you might be able to cut down on so you can reach your saving goals.

Monday

Expense	Cost
Total:	

Tuesday

Expense	Cost
Total:	

Wednesday

Expense	Cost
Total:	

Thursday

Expense	Cost
Total:	

Friday

Expense	Cost
Total:	

Saturday

Expense	Cost
Total:	

Sunday

Expense	Cost
Total:	

Notes

Things To Cut Down

Expense	Potential Saving

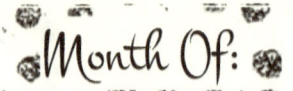

Month Of: _____ / 20

Income

	Expected	Actual
Income #1 (after tax)		
Income #2 (after tax)		
Other (after tax)		

Expenses

	Budgeted	Actual
Travel (fuel/bus/train)		
Totals		
	Leftover	

My Monthly Saving

Goal	Actual	Notes

One Off Expenses This Month

Expense	Cost	Due

Planned Treats

Treat	Budgeted	Actual Cost	Date

Totals

Money in	Money Out	Money Leftover

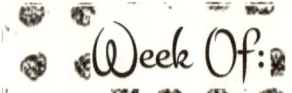

Week Of: / 20

Track everything you spend each day. This will help you see things you might be able to cut down on so you can reach your saving goals.

Monday

Expense	Cost
Total:	

Tuesday

Expense	Cost
Total:	

Wednesday

Expense	Cost
Total:	

Thursday

Expense	Cost
Total:	

Friday

Expense	Cost
Total:	

Saturday

Expense	Cost
Total:	

Sunday

Expense	Cost
Total:	

Notes

Things To Cut Down

Expense	Potential Saving

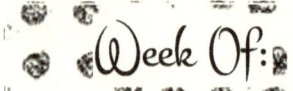

Week Of: _____ / 20

Track everything you spend each day. This will help you see things you might be able to cut down on so you can reach your saving goals.

Monday

Expense	Cost
Total:	

Tuesday

Expense	Cost
Total:	

Wednesday

Expense	Cost
Total:	

Thursday

Expense	Cost
Total:	

Friday

Expense	Cost
Total:	

Saturday

Expense	Cost
Total:	

Sunday

Expense	Cost
Total:	

Notes

Things To Cut Down

Expense	Potential Saving

Track everything you spend each day. This will help you see things you might be able to cut down on so you can reach your saving goals.

Monday

Expense	Cost
Total:	

Tuesday

Expense	Cost
Total:	

Wednesday

Expense	Cost
Total:	

Thursday

Expense	Cost
Total:	

Friday

Expense	Cost
Total:	

Saturday

Expense	Cost
Total:	

Sunday

Expense	Cost
Total:	

Notes

Things To Cut Down

Expense	Potential Saving

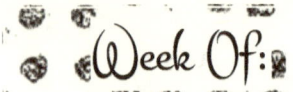

Week Of:

Track everything you spend each day. This will help you see things you might be able to cut down on so you can reach your saving goals.

Monday

Expense	Cost
Total:	

Tuesday

Expense	Cost
Total:	

Wednesday

Expense	Cost
Total:	

Thursday

Expense	Cost
Total:	

Friday

Expense	Cost
Total:	

Saturday

Expense	Cost
Total:	

Sunday

Expense	Cost
Total:	

Notes

Things To Cut Down

Expense	Potential Saving

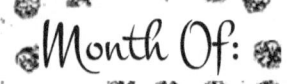 Month Of: _____ / 20

Income

	Expected	Actual
Income #1 (after tax)		
Income #2 (after tax)		
Other (after tax)		

Expenses

	Budgeted	Actual
Travel (fuel/bus/train)		
Totals		
	Leftover	

My Monthly Saving

Goal	Actual	Notes

One Off Expenses This Month

Expense	Cost	Due

Planned Treats

Treat	Budgeted	Actual Cost	Date

Totals

Money in	Money Out	Money Leftover

Track everything you spend each day. This will help you see things you might be able to cut down on so you can reach your saving goals.

Monday	
Expense	Cost
Total:	

Tuesday	
Expense	Cost
Total:	

Wednesday	
Expense	Cost
Total:	

Thursday	
Expense	Cost
Total:	

Friday

Expense	Cost
Total:	

Saturday

Expense	Cost
Total:	

Sunday

Expense	Cost
Total:	

Notes

| |
| |
| |
| |
| |
| |

Things To Cut Down

Expense	Potential Saving

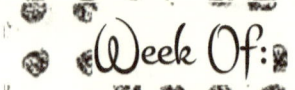

Week Of: / 20

Track everything you spend each day. This will help you see things you
might be able to cut down on so you can reach your saving goals.

Monday

Expense	Cost
Total:	

Tuesday

Expense	Cost
Total:	

Wednesday

Expense	Cost
Total:	

Thursday

Expense	Cost
Total:	

Friday

Expense	Cost
Total:	

Saturday

Expense	Cost
Total:	

Sunday

Expense	Cost
Total:	

Notes

Things To Cut Down

Expense	Potential Saving

 Week Of:

Track everything you spend each day. This will help you see things you might be able to cut down on so you can reach your saving goals.

Monday

Expense	Cost
Total:	

Tuesday

Expense	Cost
Total:	

Wednesday

Expense	Cost
Total:	

Thursday

Expense	Cost
Total:	

Friday

Expense	Cost
Total:	

Saturday

Expense	Cost
Total:	

Sunday

Expense	Cost
Total:	

Notes

Things To Cut Down

Expense	Potential Saving

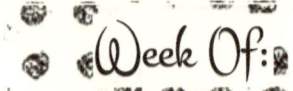

Week Of: _____ / 20

Track everything you spend each day. This will help you see things you might be able to cut down on so you can reach your saving goals.

Monday

Expense	Cost
Total:	

Tuesday

Expense	Cost
Total:	

Wednesday

Expense	Cost
Total:	

Thursday

Expense	Cost
Total:	

Friday

Expense	Cost
Total:	

Saturday

Expense	Cost
Total:	

Sunday

Expense	Cost
Total:	

Notes

Things To Cut Down

Expense	Potential Saving

Twelve Month Review

When I think about money, I feel...

_____

_____

_____

Saved So Far

Average Daily Spend

Average Monthly Spend

Things I've Cut Down On

Expense	Old Cost	Cost now

www.ingramcontent.com/pod-product-compliance
Lightning Source LLC
Chambersburg PA
CBHW022008170526
45157CB00003B/1191